# DWAYNE JOHNSON

## FAMOUS ENTERTAINER

DENNIS ST. SAUVER

BIG BUDDY POP BIOGRAPHIES

Big Buddy Books
An Imprint of Abdo Publishing
abdobooks.com

**abdobooks.com**

Published by Abdo Publishing, a division of ABDO, PO Box 398166, Minneapolis, Minnesota 55439.

Big Buddy Books™ is a trademark and logo of Abdo Publishing.

Printed in the United States of America, North Mankato, Minnesota.
102018
012019

THIS BOOK CONTAINS RECYCLED MATERIALS

Cover Photo: Jeff Spicer/Getty Images.
Interior Photos: Alberto E. Rodriguez/Getty Images (p. 23); Charley Gallay/Getty Images (p. 27); Christopher Polk/Getty Images (p. 6); Emmanuel Wong/Getty Images (p. 29); Entertainment Pictures/Alamy Stock Photo (p. 21); Ethan Miller/Getty Images (p. 17); Jason Kirk/Getty Images (p. 15); Jed Jacobsohn/Getty Images (p. 9); Kevin Winter/Getty Images (p. 25); Matt Winkelmeyer/Getty Images (p. 5); Stephen Lovekin/Getty Images (p. 19); Taylor Hill/Getty Images (p. 13); ZUMA Press, Inc./Alamy Stock Photo (p. 11).

Coordinating Series Editor: Tamara L. Britton
Contributing Series Editor: Jill M. Roesler
Graphic Design: Jenny Christensen, Cody Laberda

Library of Congress Control Number: 2018948438

Publisher's Cataloging-in-Publication Data

Names: St. Sauver, Dennis, author.
Title: Dwayne Johnson / by Dennis St. Sauver.
Description: Minneapolis, Minnesota : Abdo Publishing, 2019 | Series: Big buddy pop biographies set 4 | Includes online resources and index.
Identifiers: ISBN 9781532118005 (lib. bdg.) | ISBN 9781532171048 (ebook)
Subjects: LCSH: Johnson, Dwayne, 1972- --Juvenile literature. | Actors--United States--Biography--Juvenile literature. | Wrestlers--Biography--Juvenile literature. | Motion picture actors and actresses--Biography--Juvenile literature.
Classification: DDC 792.028092 [B]--dc23

# CONTENTS

# SUPERSTAR ACTOR

Dwayne Johnson is one of the top male movie stars in Hollywood, California. Many know him for his action movies.

He wanted to be an actor at an early age. When he was eight years old, he saw the movie *Raiders of the Lost Ark*. He liked the idea of being an action movie hero.

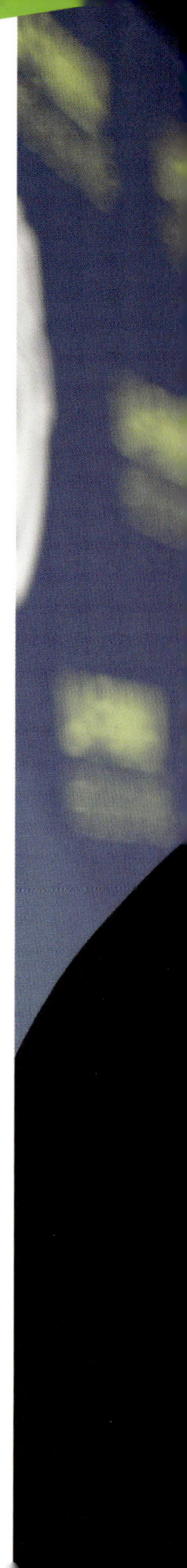

# SNAPSHOT

**NAME:**
Dwayne Douglas Johnson

**BIRTHDAY:**
May 2, 1972

**BIRTHPLACE:**
Hayward, California

**POPULAR MOVIES:**
*Jumanji: Welcome to the Jungle, Journey 2: The Mysterious Island, Moana, The Game Plan*

# FAMILY TIES

Dwayne Douglas Johnson was born in Hayward, California, on May 2, 1972. He is the son of Ata and Rocky Johnson.

The actor has three daughters. They are Simone Alexandra, 17, Jasmine, 3, and newborn Tiana.

Dwayne has been dating singer Lauren Hashian since 2007.

WHERE IN THE WORLD?
Oregon
Nevada
Hayward
PACIFIC OCEAN
California
Arizona
MEXICO
N
W
E
S

# EARLY YEARS

When Dwayne was in high school, he became a very talented football player. He even earned a **scholarship** from the University of Miami to play football.

He may have made it as a **professional** football player. But he had too many shoulder and knee **injuries**.

**DID YOU KNOW?**
Dwayne's father and grandfather were professional wrestlers.

Dwayne lived in 13 different states by the end of junior high school. He often had to attend new schools and make new friends.

# WRESTLING CAREER

When Dwayne was 24 years old, he joined World Wrestling Entertainment (WWE). His original wrestling name was Rocky Maivia.

He later joined a group called the "Nation of **Domination**." There, he became the leader of the group and continued wrestling. Fans knew him by his new nickname, "The Rock."

Dwayne became a professional wrestler instead of a football player. He was nicknamed "The Rock" because of his size and strength.

The Rock went on to win 17 major wrestling titles throughout his **career**. Many consider him one of the greatest **professional** wrestlers of all time.

He continues to make special wrestling appearances. But he now **focuses** mainly on his acting career.

**DID YOU KNOW?**

Dwayne once said, "No matter who you are, being kind is the easiest thing you can do."

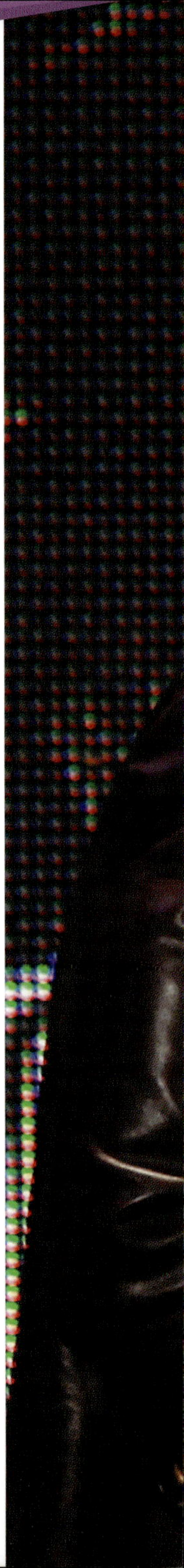

The Rock and John Cena *(right)* were rivals in WWE. Now as actors, the two are friends.

# BIG BREAK

Dwayne's **career** changed in the late 1990s. In 1999, he wrote a book about himself called *The Rock Says*. Two years later, he appeared in the hit movie *The Mummy Returns*.

He continued to work hard on his acting career. He soon became one of the biggest stars in Hollywood.

*The Mummy Returns* was a very successful movie. It marked the beginning of Dwayne's acting career.

In 2004, Dwayne stopped wrestling full-time to **focus** on acting. Since then, he has starred in science fiction, action, and family movies. He has also appeared in several TV shows. He is a very **versatile** actor!

**DID YOU KNOW?**

Dwayne eats six or seven meals a day!

In 2012, Dwayne earned the Action Star of the Year Award from CinemaCon, USA.

# COMEDY ACTOR

In addition to action movies, Dwayne has starred in several **comedies**. In 2008, he played a secret agent in the comedy *Get Smart*.

Two years later, he starred in *The Tooth Fairy*. And in 2016, he showed off his talents alongside Kevin Hart in the movie *Central Intelligence*.

Dwayne is always trying to improve as an actor. He even works with an acting coach to get better.

# MOANA

The 2016 Disney movie *Moana* was Dwayne's first **animated** film. It was also his first time singing in a movie. He was nervous to sing. But he tried his best and succeeded!

The main character, Moana, is a young Polynesian girl. She reminds Dwayne of his oldest daughter. She is **ambitious** and has her own strong views.

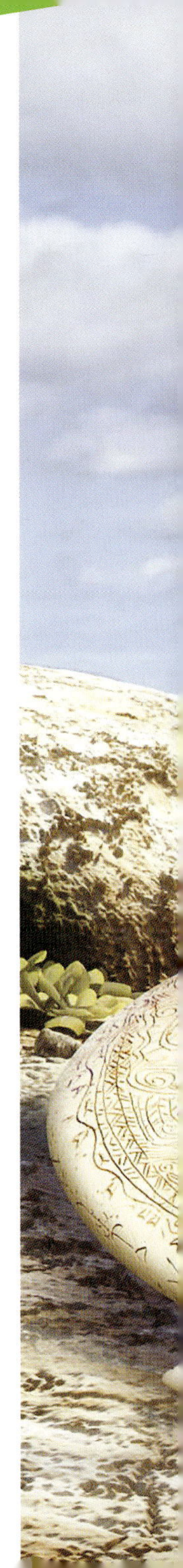

Disney did not hold tryouts for the part of Maui in the movie *Moana*. They wanted Dwayne to be the voice from the start.

Dwayne's *Moana* character Maui was partly based on Dwayne's grandfather. He was a Samoan chief named Peter Maivia. Peter was also a **professional** wrestler!

## DID YOU KNOW?

Dwayne sings the song "You're Welcome" in the movie *Moana*. He gives his mother the credit for his good singing voice.

Famous songwriter Lin-Manuel Miranda (right) composed the song "You're Welcome" for the film.

# AWARDS

Throughout his **career**, Dwayne has been **nominated** for more than 40 **awards**. And in total, he has won 11 major awards.

In 2017, he earned the People's Choice Award for Favorite **Series** Actor. That year, he also earned a star on the Hollywood Walk of Fame.

In 2018, The Rock won the Kids' Choice Award for Favorite Movie Actor. The award was for his part in *Jumanji: Welcome to the Jungle*.

# GIVING BACK

Dwayne takes time to help out with many different **foundations**. One of those is the Beacon Experience. It is a program to help kids finish high school.

He also supports causes that work toward ending illnesses called Parkinson's disease and AIDS. And sometimes he reaches out to his fans to show support.

Dwayne also runs The Rock Foundation. Through his foundation, children who are in hospitals can get the help they need.

# BUZZ

Dwayne is very popular across the world. He is always busy filming movies and TV shows. Fans can expect to see The Rock on the big screen for years to come!

**DID YOU KNOW?**
The Rock is planning a new TV game show. It will be called *The Titan Games*.

Dwayne thought about running for President of the United States in 2020. But he said that he is no longer considering it.

# GLOSSARY

**ambitious** possessing a desire for success, honor, or power.

**animated** appearing to be alive or moving.

**award** something that is given in recognition of good work or a good act.

**career** a period of time spent in a certain job.

**comedy** a funny story.

**domination** to have a commanding position or controlling power over.

**focus** (FOH-kuhs) to give attention to.

**foundation** (faun-DAY-shuhn) an organization that controls gifts of money and services.

**injury** (IHNJ-ree) hurt or loss received.

**nominate** to name as a possible winner.

**professional** (pruh-FEHSH-nuhl) working for money rather than only for pleasure.

**scholarship** money or aid given to help a student continue his or her studies.

**series** a set of similar things or events in order.

**versatile** able to do many different kinds of things.

## ONLINE RESOURCES

Booklinks
NONFICTION NETWORK
FREE! ONLINE NONFICTION RESOURCES

To learn more about Dwayne Johnson, visit **abdobooklinks.com**. These links are routinely monitored and updated to provide the most current information available.

# INDEX